WONDER OF WONDERS: MAN

Secrets of the Heart and Blood

A million years ago,
Man appeared on earth...

A creature without fangs or claws, without hoofs or horns, without scales or fur. How did he compete with the animals? By what means did he come to be master of the earth?

From pole to pole, from east to west, Man is lord of all he surveys. He has harnessed the rivers, created new lakes, watered the deserts, cut continents apart. His ships outswim the whale, his cars outrun the cheetah, his planes outfly the falcon. The smoke of his factories darkens the sky. He is dwarfed by his own buildings, he is lost in the maze of his own highways.

How did this happen?

The answer lies in Man's wonderful body and mind, Nature's highest achievement. It is *by means* of his body and mind and *for the sake* of his body and mind that Man has subdued the animals, mastered the plants, invented the arts, explored the earth, split the atom.

This is the glorious story told in the series WONDER OF WONDERS: MAN.

WONDER OF WONDERS: MAN

Secrets of the Heart and Blood

By Anne Terry White
and Gerald S. Lietz, M.D.

Illustrated by Ted Schroeder

GARRARD PUBLISHING COMPANY
CHAMPAIGN, ILLINOIS

Photo credits:

The Bettmann Archive: pp. 25, 68, 71, 79
Wide World: p. 74

Contents

1
Seventy-Two Times a Minute

Who isn't proud to live in this age of great machines? Who doesn't feel a little bit taller because Man has built such wonders?

But let us not boast. There is something Man can never build: He will never make a machine as wonderful as himself. For what thing made of metal, plastic, rubber, glass, and electric cord can compare with that wonder of wonders, Man? The human body is a machine that builds itself. It stokes and regulates itself. It repairs itself. And long before it wears out, it creates new machines to take its place.

Man is as curious as a monkey—he wants to find out how everything works. It must have been ages ago that he first began to wonder about his body.

Doubtless one of the first things man wondered about was his blood. We can see him now, staring in awe and terror the first time he beheld the red liquid spurting from a wound. We can imagine how his heart pounded and how he dimly wondered what thing it was that beat like a bird against his ribs.

Man has been wondering about his blood and heart ever since. He has worked hard to solve their mysteries. But he doesn't know everything yet. He doesn't yet understand all that the blood contains. He doesn't know yet what makes the heart beat.

Thump. Thump. What starts that pump inside us going? What keeps it pumping on an average of 72 times a minute over a lifetime of seventy years or more? Where does the heart get its orders?

You can say to your muscles, "Raise the right arm." The message will be carried from the brain along a nerve, and the muscles will do your bidding. But your heart will not mind you. When you are frightened, or excited, and your heart begins to pound, there is no use saying to it, "Sit still, my beating heart, sit still." There is no "wire" along which your message can be carried. No nerve goes from the brain to the heart. So the heart acts independently. It seems to tell itself to beat.

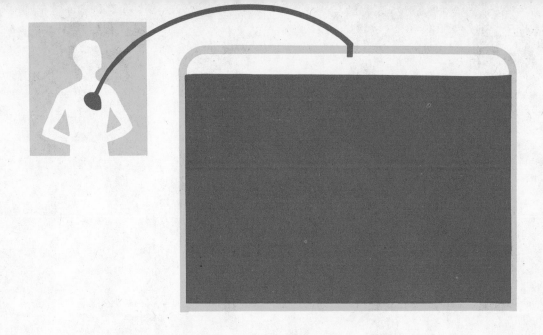

The body contains 5–6 quarts of blood, yet the heart pumps 3,000 gallons of blood each day. It is the same blood pumped over and over.

It is all so mysterious. The pump is just a bundle of muscle not much bigger than your fist. It weighs only about ten ounces. Is it not strange that so small a thing should be so important to the body? You can lose both your arms and legs, and live. You can lose three-fourths of your stomach, several feet of your intestines, half your lungs, and still live. But when the heart stops beating, that is the end. When the heart stops, life stops with it.

Why?

Because then the blood can no longer go about its work. When the heart stops, the blood cannot move.

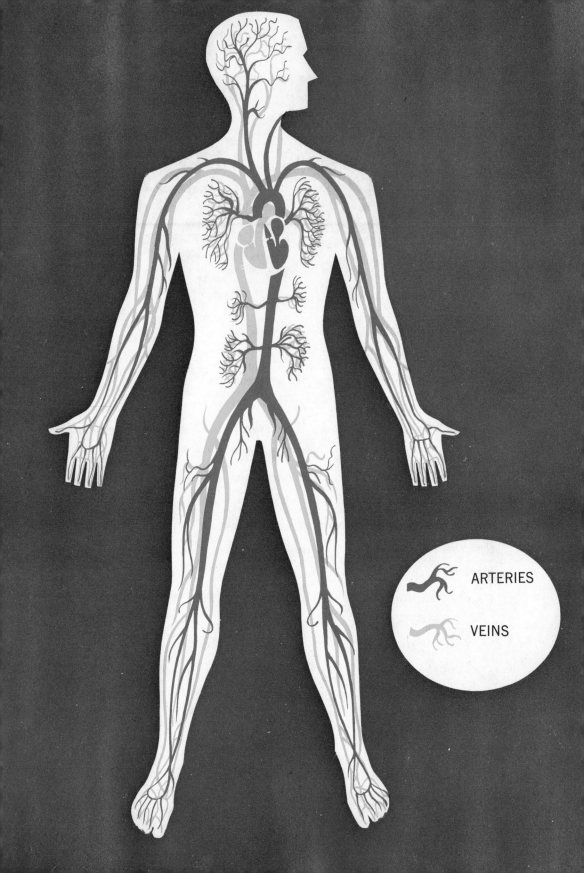

ARTERIES

VEINS

It stops carrying food and oxygen to the body. It stops taking its waste away. And without these services, the eyes cannot see, the lungs cannot breathe, the brain cannot think, the muscles cannot contract.

We might compare the body to a great city. The blood vessels are its highways, streets, and alleys. The body's millions upon millions of tiny parts, which we call cells, are the houses. Now, life in each house needs many things—food, water, fresh air, heat, and so on. Each house must have its garbage and ashes and trash and sewage removed. In a great city like New York, hundreds of trains and ships and barges and thousands of trucks are needed to service the houses. Rivers, miles and miles of sewers, and millions of miles of water pipes share in the work.

In the body nearly all the carrying is done by the blood. The blood is both a delivery and a pickup service. It travels in a sort of circle—out from the heart to all the body by way of the arteries, back to the heart by way of the veins.

And the heart?

The heart is the wonderful pump that sends the service on its way. The heart keeps the life stream flowing.

2

The Meaning of "Lub-Dub"

We are frequently told that the heart is on the left side of the body. But it isn't. It is only slanted a little to the left. To locate your heart, place the palm of your left hand over your chest. Feel around for the thumping—it will be near the left breast. When you have found it, put the hollow part of your palm over the heartbeat. Your fingers will point toward the center of your throat, and your hand will be in the same position as the heart underneath.

The heart partly lies and partly hangs just under the ribs. Naturally, so important an organ must not be allowed to rub against the body. So the heart is

loosely covered by a sack—much like a plastic bag—
and the space between heart and sack is filled with a
slippery fluid.

To see the true shape of the heart, you must forget
about valentines. The heart is shaped like a pear—one
that is hollow inside. It stands to reason that it must
be hollow, for a solid heart could hold no blood. But
the walls of the pear are pretty thick—in some places
as thick as a slice of bread, in others the thickness
of orange rind. What is more, the muscle of the
heart is peculiar. In the whole body there is no other
like it. It is very tough. And the muscle strips are
arranged in a special way. They wind around in all
directions, much the same way yarn is wound into
a hollow ball.

Now, all muscle has just one job in life—to
contract, that is, to pull itself shorter. And the work
of the strong, tough heart muscle is just this—to
contract. It contracts with a jerk. Then it relaxes
and goes back to its old shape. It is like squeezing
your fist tight and then letting it relax. Each time
the heart contracts, there is a heartbeat. In between
the beats, the heart rests. If you add up the time
between beats, you will find that the heart rests ten
hours a day. That surely helps to keep the pump in

good condition. And well that it does, for this flesh-and-blood pump can take no time out for repairs—if it stops pumping, the body will die.

All normal hearts beat as regularly as a clock ticks. But size seems to have something to do with the rate. A baby's heart beats 120 times a minute. A man's heart beats 72, while the huge elephant's heart beats only 25 times a minute.

However, though the heart beats regularly, it doesn't always beat at the same speed. This you can easily prove.

Put your hand tightly over your heart and count the number of thumps in one minute. Or take your pulse—that is, count the beats in one minute—at the wrist. There is a hidden artery there. It is on the palm side of your wrist where the thumb joins it. In this artery you can feel the blood being pumped into your hand.

Now jump up and down ten times and count again. You will find that your heart beats faster after the jumping. But sit still a few minutes and count again. Once more the heart is beating slowly. It is again pumping about five pints a minute. If you had done something more violent than jumping—run a race, for instance—the heart would have thumped

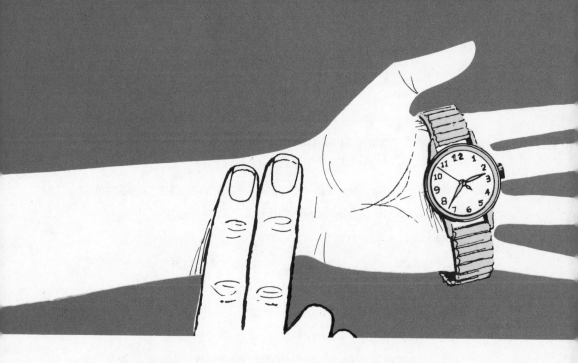

even faster. It might have pumped several *gallons* of blood a minute to help you win the race.

You might ask why. Why did the heart beat faster when you jumped? It seems quite unbelievable, but it is as though the heart *knew* that more oxygen was needed by those jumping legs of yours. It got a signal to pump faster. You didn't know your legs needed more oxygen. Yet the heart mysteriously got a signal.

Doctors have studied and studied the beating of the heart. They have drawn countless diagrams to explain how it works. What would you see if doctors were to show you an animated cartoon of it?

15

First you would see the top half of the pump contracting. In much less than a second you would see the bottom half contracting. The beating heart would seem to rock like a seesaw.

Because the two contractions come so close together, to us they feel like one thump. But that isn't a true report of what goes on. When the doctor listens to the heart with his instrument, he hears something different. To him the heartbeat sounds like "lub-dub, lub-dub, lub-dub."

Now, what is the reason?

The reason is that the heart is really not one pump, but two. The heart is like a four-room duplex house, with two rooms on each side. One room is upstairs, one down—the *auricle* above and the *ventricle* below. The two rooms on the right are separated from the two rooms on the left by a wall. Though they are side by side, the two halves of the duplex house are absolutely private—there is no door between them. But each upstairs and downstairs is one unit. So there *is* communication between them. A door opens out of each auricle and leads into the ventricle below. The door opens only one way, from upstairs down. Whatever comes down has to stay down; it can't go back up.

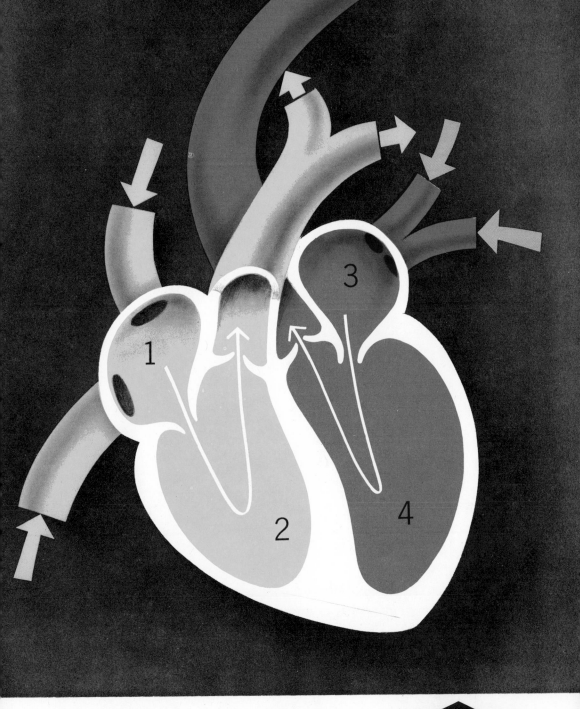

The yellow color shows how blood from the body goes to room 1 of the heart, on to room 2 and to the lungs. The red color shows blood entering room 3, being pumped to room 4, and out to the body again.

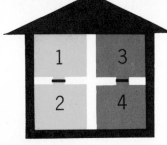

An animated cartoon would show the inside of the pump working like this:

First, the two top rooms contract. As they do so, the blood from each auricle is squeezed into its ventricle. This is step one.

Step two is that each ventricle squeezes its blood out of the heart and sends it on its way. And just as the ventricle contracts, the door leading down from the auricle closes with a bang.

Step 1

Step 2

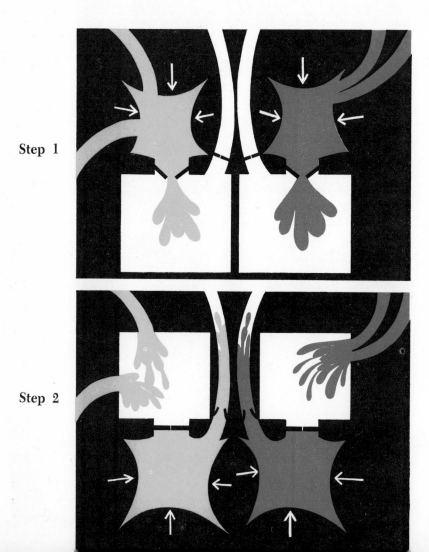

That is why the doctor listening to the heartbeat hears "lub-dub." He is hearing each half of the heart as it contracts. He is hearing two sets of doors slam.

Now what need is there for two sides of the heart? What is the pump built like that for?

You may be sure there is a good reason for it. Nature did a lot of experimenting before she arrived at a heart that is a duplex house. Jellyfish have no heart at all. Fishes have a heart with only two rooms, and snakes have a heart with three. Only the higher animals—mammals and birds—have a heart that is a four-room duplex.

Pure blood is the reason for our four-room duplex house. You will remember that we said the blood is both a delivery and a pickup service. It goes out to the body loaded with food and oxygen, and bright red in color. It comes back dark, of a bluish color—you can see how blue it is in the veins. It is loaded with waste now. Well, this impure blue blood must not be allowed to mix with the pure red blood in the heart. And it doesn't, for there is the solid wall between the two sides.

The blood carrying waste from the body comes flowing into the right side of the heart. It is pumped out at once to the lungs to get purified. There it gives up the carbon dioxide it has been carrying and takes on a load of oxygen. Then the blood returns to the heart. It comes back to the left side where the pure blood is, and now the two can safely mix.

That sounds complicated. It *is* complicated. But the whole thing takes place amazingly fast. A drop of blood makes its trip through the four rooms of the heart in 20 seconds. It takes just one-third of a minute for a drop to go from the right auricle to the right ventricle, out to the lungs, back to the left auricle, into the left ventricle, and out to the body again.

But the blood leaving the left ventricle goes to every part of the body. It goes even to the teeth, even to the bones. How much time does that take? How long does it take for the blood to go to the farthest part of the body—the toes, say—and come back to the heart?

Just two minutes.

It makes one dizzy to think about it. It is hard to realize that this rapid-transit delivery and pickup service is actually inside us. It is unbelievable that this service goes about its business day after day, twenty-four hours a day, three hundred and sixty-five days a year for perhaps seventy years and more.

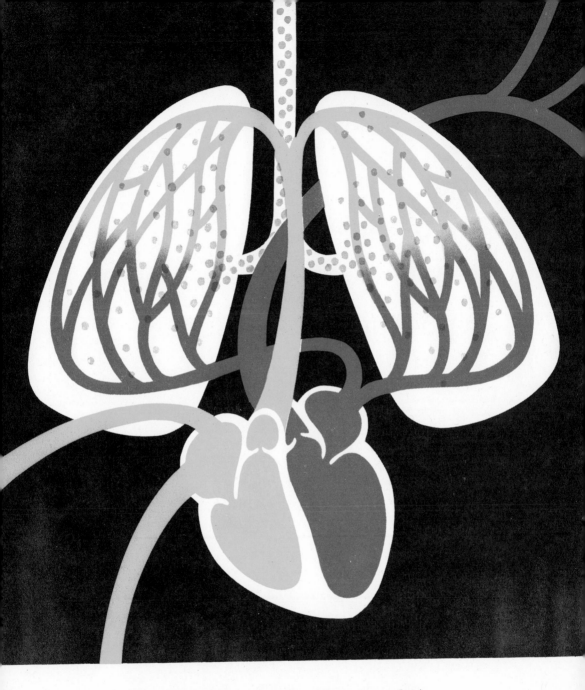

With each breath you take, oxygen (grey dots) comes down the windpipe and enters the lungs. Impure blood enters the tiny vessels of the lungs and picks up this oxygen. This purer blood returns to the heart where it is pumped out to nourish the body.

3

"A Motion, as it Were, in a Circle"

It took astronomers a long time to understand that the earth moves round the sun. Most of the world didn't believe Copernicus and Galileo when they said it was so. To save his life, Galileo took back his words.

Anatomists floundered a long time before they understood the workings of the heart. It took them many centuries to realize that the blood goes round to the parts of the body and comes back to the heart. When Dr. William Harvey proved that it was so, a great many people wouldn't believe it.

That was in the early 1600's.

William Harvey was an English lad who wanted to be a doctor. British schools at that time, however, were far behind Italy in the teaching of medicine. So when he got through college, he went abroad and entered the University of Padua. Great scientists were teaching there. Galileo was one. Fabricius was another. Harvey studied anatomy under Fabricius.

The professor had written about every part of the body of animals except the heart, the blood vessels, and the blood. But he had carefully studied the blood system and had even made a discovery there. He had cut open a vein and seen little valves inside it. They were like tiny, very delicate half-moons. He didn't know what the valves were for, but he pointed them out to his students. Perhaps one of them would some day find out the meaning of the valves.

Now, in those days the most learned physicians had the weirdest notions about the heart and blood. Even the great Fabricius said the heart and arteries "pulsed" in order to fan and *refrigerate* the blood. Some said just the opposite. They said the heart was the workshop where *heat* was made. Or they said it was the place where the "spirits" were born. The arteries were supposed to carry the "spirits" around to all parts of the body that needed them, and the

23

veins carried food. Many believed the arteries held blood and air mixed, or else only air. However, the favorite idea was that the blood went back and forth along the same blood vessels. It moved, the doctors said, like the rise and fall of the tides.

Young William Harvey was soon familiar with all these theories. But, like Galileo, he refused to take anybody's word for the way things worked. Harvey believed in finding out for himself. He meant to experiment.

If he had lived some fifty years earlier, Harvey might have been saved a lot of work. For he might have learned something about the way the blood really moves from the Spaniard, Miguel Servetus. This man had actually grasped one of the great secrets of the heart. He understood that the blood goes from one side of the heart to the lungs and comes back to the other side. He described the motion in a book. But unfortunately, Servetus was burned at the stake and all copies of his book except one were burned with him. Since the last book was kept by one of his judges, Harvey had to start from scratch.

As soon as he got back to his own country and started to practice medicine, he experimented. Naturally, he couldn't cut open his patients to see how their hearts and blood worked. So he cut open frogs, lizards, snakes, pigeons, turtles, small fishes, pigs, and dogs. At first he understood nothing. He couldn't make out what happened when the heart beat. It happened in the twinkling of an eye, it came and went like a flash of lightning. Harvey was so confused by what he saw, or thought he saw, that he began to believe the motion of the heart "could be understood only by God."

Amazed friends watch while Dr. William Harvey demonstrates the circulation of the blood.

Still he kept on trying. And at last he could see that on the beat the heart grew firm, tense, and paler in color. He understood then that on the beat the muscle contracted and the blood was squeezed out. It was the contraction that felt like a thump.

One of the things which puzzled the doctor was the large quantity of blood that the heart pumped out. When he dissected a human corpse, he sometimes found as much as two ounces of blood in the left ventricle. Was this how much the heart sent out into the body each time it beat? If so, there was a problem. Even supposing that only one-eighth as much was squeezed out, still there was a problem. For that blood would add up to a fantastic amount in just an hour's time. In a single hour the heart might beat anywhere from four to five thousand times. That meant that the left ventricle pumped out in one short hour more blood than the whole body contained!

What was the answer?

The doctor saw that there could be only one. The heart pumped the *same* blood over and over again. The blood went out of the heart *and came back to it.* There was "a motion, as it were, in a circle." The blood went to the body by way of the arteries. It came back by way of the veins. He could easily prove this. For if he put a tight bandage around the arm, the artery would instantly swell up *above* the bandage, and there would be no pulse at the wrist. Clearly the blood coming *from* the heart had been shut off. At the same time the vein *below* the bandage would swell. The blood was being stopped on its way back *to* the heart.

And those valves, those delicate valves shaped like a half-moon—he understood them now. They were tiny folding doors that opened only one way. They were set in the veins to prevent blood from going back into the arteries. Not a single drop could flow back—the doors were tight-shut against it. The blood *had* to go on in the direction of the heart.

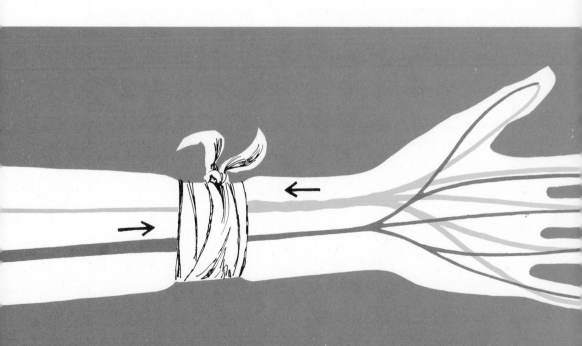

All this was so new, so unheard-of, that William Harvey hesitated to put it down in a book. He knew that people hate to change their ideas. "I tremble," he said when his friends urged him to write, "lest I have mankind at large for my enemies."

But had he a right to keep his discoveries to himself? The heart to the body was like the sun to the world. All growth, all power came from it. The heart was like the prince in a kingdom; it ruled over all. His discovery was too important to hide.

So at last Harvey began to write. "The die is cast," he said. "My trust is in my love of truth."

He called his book *On the Motion of the Heart and Blood in Animals.*

Of course, just what he expected happened. When people read his book, or were told what it said, they were shocked and outraged. "Just who is this crack-brained young upstart?" they demanded. "How dare he dispute what the great physicians of the past have said?" Scientists sent him insulting letters. His practice fell off badly.

It was fortunate for Harvey that men were no longer burned at the stake for cutting up a corpse.

4

Malpighi Looks Through the Microscope

Twenty or thirty years passed before doctors came to their senses. But when they did, and realized what Harvey had done for them, they began to feel the way navigators had felt when they got the compass. They weren't lost in a fog any more, for they had something to steer by.

William Harvey had made the greatest discovery that has *ever* been made about the human body. And yet something was missing. There was one single step in the journey of the blood which he had not found out. *How did the blood get from the arteries into the veins?*

The arteries started out from the heart like the trunk of a tree. Blood went out to the body by a great vessel that was an inch across. The trunk soon divided. The branches broke up into smaller and smaller branches, and these, in turn, broke up into twigs. But between the smallest twigs of the arteries and the smallest twigs of the veins there was a gap. How did the blood bridge that gap? Harvey had looked and looked through his magnifying glass at the space between. Though everything was several times bigger, he still couldn't see any bridges. "It must be," he decided, "that from the smallest branches of the arteries, the blood flows directly into the pores of the flesh. And from these pores it makes its way into the smallest branches of the veins."

He had to leave it at that.

But it didn't stay there. In the very year that Harvey's book came out, another genius was born in Italy. He was Marcello Malpighi. And he was not only a genius, but a lucky one, for by the time he was grown, the microscope had been developed. Malpighi could enter an invisible world. He could behold what was too small for the naked eye to see.

He made pictures of the delicate insides of a silk-worm. He drew the tiny air tubes which carry air to

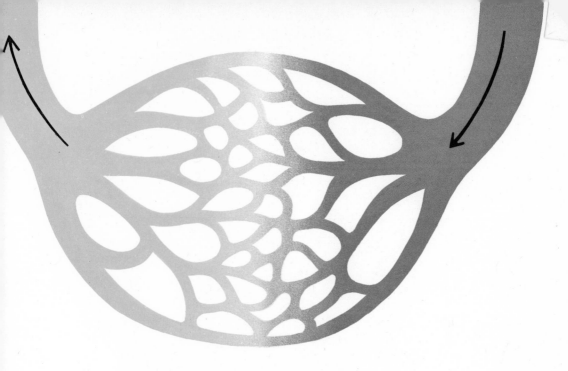

Blood from the artery enters this capillary, releases its oxygen, picks up carbon dioxide, and passes on to the vein.

every nook and corner of an insect's body. One day he turned his microscope on a bit of a frog's lung and saw what Harvey had tried so hard to see.

The space between the smallest arteries and the smallest veins in the frog's lung was not empty. A network of still smaller channels filled it. They joined the arteries to the veins in a ring-like fashion. The channels looked like so many hairs, but, of course, that was a great exaggeration. If the microscope showed them that big, they were actually many times smaller. But the name *capillaries,* "hair-like," would do.

31

How about the blood itself? What would that look like under the microscope?

Blood was a mystery. It was something that people had looked upon with awe from earliest times. It was something that aroused their deepest feelings. "Blood is the life," the Bible said. Blood must not be eaten. Blood was sacred.

Many emotions surrounded the blood. And from these emotions ideas sprang up. The first law of the tribe was the law of "blood revenge." That meant that if anyone killed a member of the tribe, the tribe was obliged to kill the murderer or a member of his family. "Blood" made all members of the tribe brothers. If a man became friends with one who was not of his tribe, the two could become brothers by an exchange of blood. They made what was called a "blood bond." They gashed their arms and each sucked some of the other's blood. After that their tie was as close as though they were sons of the same father and mother.

Blood was something that gave a person status. A man was of "good blood" if he came from a noble family. He was of "bad blood" if his father had committed a crime. Best of all was to be of "royal blood." That was next best to being divine.

Now, the heart beats faster when we are excited. So it was natural for people to suppose that emotion springs from the heart. A quick-tempered person was said to be "hot-blooded." A person who killed without mercy was a "cold-blooded" murderer. And when two people had a long-lasting quarrel, it was said that there was "bad blood" between them.

"Blood is thicker than water," people said, meaning that members of a family will stand up for and help one another. But if blood really was thicker than water, what made it so? No one knew. No one had tried to find out. Blood was simply a red fluid.

People knew that blood would clot. They saw that blood coming from an artery was brighter in color than blood coming from a vein. And they supposed that blood did some important things in the body. But what those things were, nobody knew. Doctors were so confused about it that they thought the best way to cure sick people was to bleed them. It did not matter why they were sick. Every physician carried a lancet with which to cut open a vein to "let" blood. Some people were professional "blood-letters." They attached leeches to the patient and let the creatures suck out blood. Indeed, after a time the blood-letters themselves came to be called leeches.

A great many patients were helped to the grave by this senseless treatment. But if they did happen to recover in spite of it, it was supposed that the bleeding had cured them of their illness.

Malpighi turned his microscope on human blood....

Four years after he discovered the capillaries, the Italian unveiled the first of the blood's secrets. Blood was not a simple red liquid. It was a strange river that carried strange boats. Under the microscope he could see red blood cells floating in the stream.

It was the great beginning.

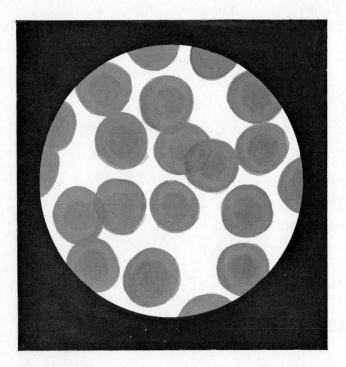

This is what Malpighi saw floating in human blood when he looked through a microscope —red blood cells.

5

A Pinched-off Bit
of the Sea

Today we know a great deal about what goes on in our blood. For many, many people have added sentences, paragraphs, and whole chapters to its wonderful story. In a hundred laboratories men and women are hard at work. Someone may come up any minute with another magnificent surprise like polio serum.

Well, then, what have we learned since Harvey told us that blood goes round and round?

Wonderful things. . . .

We have found out that blood is both a liquid and a solid, almost half and half, and that we can separate the two. If we let blood stand in a glass, the solid parts settle to the bottom, while the liquid floats to the top. We call the liquid *plasma*. Its color is the color of straw.

Plasma is more than nine-tenths just plain water. But, as Malpighi said, blood is no simple fluid. That other one-tenth teems with things that have been dissolved in the water. We can no more see them than we can see the sugar that has been dissolved in a cup of coffee. But they are there. Calcium, sodium, potassium, iron, copper are there. Iodine and phosphorus are there. All these make plasma amazingly like sea water. And there is a curious reason why this is so. *The first blood in the world was sea water.*

Let us look back a moment. Let us roll away two thousand million years and try to see what life was like when it first appeared on this planet.

There was no living creature on the land then. Everything that could be called life was in the sea. And it was very small and very simple life. The creatures in the ocean consisted of just one cell. Those creatures had no need of blood. What use was a delivery and pickup service to them when they were surrounded by water? They could get all the food and oxygen they needed out of the sea. They could let their waste out directly into the ocean.

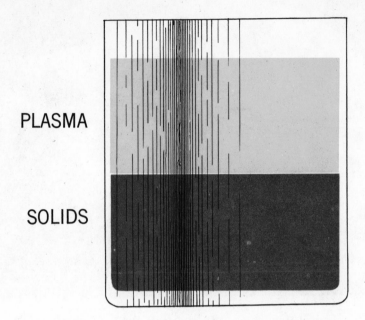

PLASMA

SOLIDS

And even when creatures with several cells developed, there was yet no need for blood. The cells were all in a row, or in two rows. Each one could still help itself to what it needed from the sea.

Difficulties arose only when animals got so big that many of their cells were on the inside, shut away from the sea water. The creatures solved the problem by canals. The sea flowed through these canals and brought food and oxygen to the cells deep inside. Sponges were creatures like that. They still are. Sponges get their food and oxygen by means of canals.

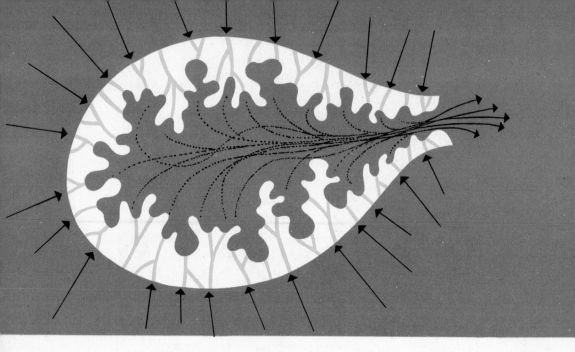

A sponge takes its food from the sea through canals, gets rid of waste at the open end.

A long, long time passed. And out of some such animal as the sponge, a new form developed. It was a creature that had *closed in around its canal.* The sea water no longer poured in at one end and out at the other. It stayed inside the animal. The outer cells got food and oxygen from the ocean and passed these, through certain openings, into the canal. The fluid in the canal became a delivery and pickup service. It fed the cells, supplied them with oxygen, and collected their waste. And it passed the waste back into the ocean through openings in the cells of the outer layer.

So the first blood stream was just a pinched-off bit of the sea. Our blood tastes salty. It has the salts of the sea in it. But the sea tastes saltier. That is because year by year more and more salts are being dissolved out of the rocks and washed into the sea. We have inside us a bit of the *original* sea.

Over millions of years our blood has changed, and become more than sea water. Besides the salts dissolved in the plasma, there are foods—sugars, fats, and proteins. These foods are dissolved in the plasma, too. Plasma contains the liquid food of the body. As the blood moves along the capillaries, food and water sift out through the very thin walls, and every cell *selects* just what it needs. At the same time the proteins thicken the blood and prevent red blood cells from leaking out. And this they surely would do, for the walls of the capillaries are made of just one single layer of body cells.

Yet plasma is much more than food and water. It contains a substance that causes blood to clot. It contains *hormones*—chemicals which control growth and other important matters. It contains *antibodies* which prevent our getting a second attack of diseases like mumps, measles, or whooping cough. It contains a world of things which we do not yet understand.

6

Transport on the Stream

Let us ask ourselves a question: Why do we eat?

"Food tastes good," we say. Yes, but that is just one of Nature's tricks. It is as much a trick as the color and odor of flowers is a trick. Nature gives flowers their beauty and smell so that bees will be attracted and will carry pollen from flower to flower as they suck the honey. Nature makes food taste good to us in order that we should be tempted to eat.

For without food we cannot live, we cannot grow. We eat and then we digest our food. That means we turn it into such form that the blood can absorb it and carry it along. In the small intestine the blood

40

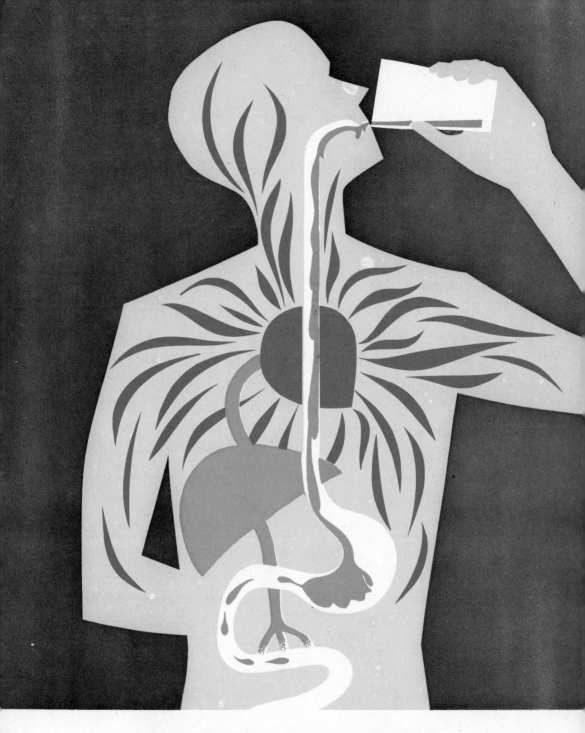

Milk goes through the stomach and intestine to be digested. Blood absorbs the digested food and carries it through the liver to the heart. This enriched blood is pumped to all the body capillaries. The digested food is used by the cells for energy.

picks up the digested food and carries it through the liver and into the heart. Finally it gets to the cells, which "burn" the digested food and make heat and energy for the body.

But body heat is something that needs control. Too much or too little will kill. Mountaineers know better than to lie down to sleep in the snow no matter how exhausted they are. They know that their body heat will not be enough to keep them from freezing. When we have a fever and the body's temperature goes up and up, we know that life is in danger. The right temperature for the human body seems to be 98.6 degrees Fahrenheit. The body keeps itself at that temperature, or very near it. The body has a built-in thermostat.

That sounds magical. But actually the thermostat is as simple as ABC.

To keep the engine of a car from getting too hot, we put water in the radiator. The water absorbs the heat and carries it off. It radiates it away. In much the same way the blood absorbs and carries off the body's heat. On a hot day the tiny blood vessels just under the skin expand. The warm blood fills them and gives its heat off through the skin. At the same time water sifts out of the little blood tubes. Little beads of perspiration form on the skin. As they evaporate, the body cools.

In cold weather just the opposite happens. Instead of being radiated away, the heat is saved. For in cold weather the little blood vessels beneath the skin are not opened so wide. Less blood comes to the skin. There is no perspiration. The heat stays in, and the body remains at 98.6 degrees Fahrenheit or thereabouts.

It is mainly this thermostat of ours that puts Man, along with other mammals and birds, into the class of "warm-blooded" animals. Other animals, like frogs or snakes, are "cold-blooded" compared to us. They

Adjusting to Heat　　　　　　　　　　　**Adjusting to Cold**

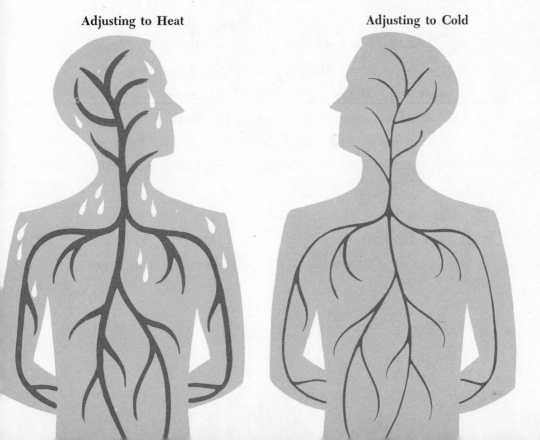

cannot keep an even temperature. How warm they are depends on the warmth of their surroundings. To fishes this doesn't matter because down under the surface of the ocean, each latitude stays pretty much at the same temperature day and night, summer and winter. But to the land-living, cold-blooded animals, it makes a big difference. For the air does not stay at the same temperature. As the weather gets colder in the temperate zone, the amphibia and reptiles get sluggish. To keep their blood from freezing, they have to do something about it. They have to move to a warmer climate, or they have to hibernate.

Our thermostat extends our world. Mammals and birds can make their home everywhere on the earth so long as they can find food there. Polar bears can live at the North Pole. Penguins can live at the South Pole. With fur or feathers to trap and hold a layer of warm air about their bodies, mammals and birds don't need to worry about cold air. Man, to be sure, has lost most of his body hair. The clothing, however, which this wonder of wonders has invented more than makes up for it.

But let us go back to the "burning" the cells do. It is a kind of burning in which there is no flame. Still, burning of any kind calls for oxygen. You know that. You smother your campfire with ashes to put the flames out. You keep the oxygen away.

Now, living creatures had no trouble getting oxygen so long as they stayed in the sea. They took oxygen out of the water all around them. The problem of oxygen arose when they came on land and started living at the bottom of the ocean of air. They had to get oxygen out of this strange new ocean. They did it by means of a pair of lungs. Our lungs breathe in air, hold on to the oxygen, and then breathe out carbon dioxide.

But how does that oxygen get from the lungs to every part of the body?

That's where Malpighi's red blood cells come in. They are the oxygen bearers. Loaded with oxygen or carbon dioxide on the return trip, they float in the plasma like so many boats with no one to steer them. Sometimes the boats stack up, half a dozen on top of one another. In the narrow capillaries they ride slowly along, one behind another.

The red blood cells are so tiny! They can no more be seen by the naked eye than germs can. Red cells are so small that four thousand of them set side by side wouldn't measure an inch. In a single drop of blood there are many million. Perhaps there are as many as 25 trillion (25,000,000,000,000) of them in the body of the average man. Each cell is shaped like a disk that has been pressed down in the center. In fact, red blood cells look for all the world like tiny doughnuts that have not been cut all the way through.

Where do these millions and trillions come from?

They are made in the marrow of certain bones— the skull, ribs, breastbone, and the flat bones of the spine. In children they are also made at the end of the long bones of the legs and arms. Here the red blood cells grow, mature, become big enough to be used for transport, and get filled with a substance called hemoglobin. There is iron in each clump of hemoglobin. It is the combination of hemoglobin, iron, and oxygen that gives the red color to blood.

Now there is something very special about hemoglobin. It "likes" to associate with oxygen. It also "likes" to associate with carbon dioxide. So it is perfect for Nature's purpose. It is just right for carrying oxygen from the lungs to the body and carbon dioxide from the body to the lungs.

That is the sole business of the red blood cells. They load up with oxygen in the lungs, transport it, and unload it in the capillaries, through whose thin walls the oxygen seeps out to the body. In the

When red blood cells enter a body capillary, shown at the top, they give off their oxygen. Carbon dioxide is picked up and carried back to the lungs, where it is exhaled.

capillaries they load up with the carbon dioxide which has seeped in, transport it, and unload it in the lungs. They do this day and night, night and day. On the way they knock up against one another. They bump into the walls of the blood vessels. They get battered and bruised as they squeeze single file through the narrow capillaries, which are barely wide enough to let them through. The result is that the cells soon wear out. A red blood cell lasts only about 125 days. Then it dies. But new ones are always being made. Every second another two and a half million red blood cells are made in the bones. And every second about two and a half million die. They keep a nice balance.

But the body is very saving. It wastes nothing that is of value to it. Though the old, broken-down cells are taken to the liver and are there broken up, the hemoglobin with its precious atoms of iron is never thrown aside. The blood carries it right back to the bone marrow. The wonderful body machine uses it over and over again to fill the new red blood cells that are forever growing up.

7

When Blood Comes Oozing Out

Clearly red blood cells are of great importance to the body. If a person doesn't have enough of them, or if he doesn't have enough hemoglobin in each blood cell, he is in trouble. For oxygen doesn't get around to his body cells as it should. As a result, he doesn't have much energy. He is pale. And he tires easily.

Such people are said to be anemic. They get that way because their bone marrow cannot make enough red blood cells. Or perhaps the food they eat doesn't have enough iron or enough vitamins. But a person can also become anemic in another common way.

He can be in an accident and lose blood. That, alas! happens far too often nowadays when there are so many cars on the roads and all the world is in such a tearing hurry.

Everybody has had the experience of losing a *little* blood. Who hasn't stuck himself with a needle or a pin? Or cut himself with a kitchen knife? Or on a piece of broken glass? But a small cut will by no means make us anemic. The body repairs little breaks along its many miles of blood vessels very quickly. It keeps on hand all the materials necessary to take care of such accidents.

One of these materials is platelets. Like the red blood cells, platelets are solid particles floating in the plasma. But they are not cells. They are *bits* of cells, fragments of certain giant cells that scientists don't understand very well. The scientists do know, however, that these giant cells form in the bone marrow and get so big that they can't hold together. Then they break up and become platelets—tiny, flat, plate-like pieces of different shapes. Each one is about a third, or a half, as big as a red blood cell.

The body makes use of platelets in several ways, but most importantly for repair work on blood vessels. As soon as blood starts to ooze out, plasma carries platelets to the spot. They clump up around the wound, then break up. And this in turn starts chemical changes which make clotting possible. Tiny fibers settle out of the blood and build a network across the wound. Then solid parts of the blood get trapped in this network. A clot forms and plugs up the hole. The blood can't get past the clot, which quickly hardens and becomes what we call a scab. Underneath the scab, repair work goes on. And when everything is healed and the scab isn't needed any more, it falls off.

Platelets arrive quickly at the scene of a cut. They break up, causing the blood to clot. This forms a scab until the wound is repaired.

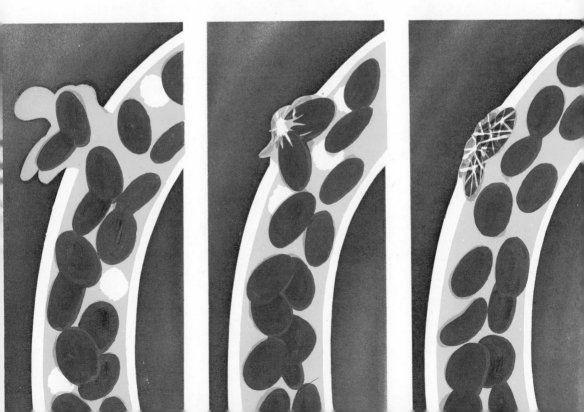

It is always a little frightening to see blood come oozing out, but to lose a little is not dangerous. We can lose even a pint of blood without harm.

Yet even that much is not quickly got back. It may take the body several weeks to build a new pint of blood. If the victim of an accident loses

Left: A transfusion. *Right top:* Blood cells of a proper transfusion. *Bottom:* Clustered cells resulting from use of wrong blood type.

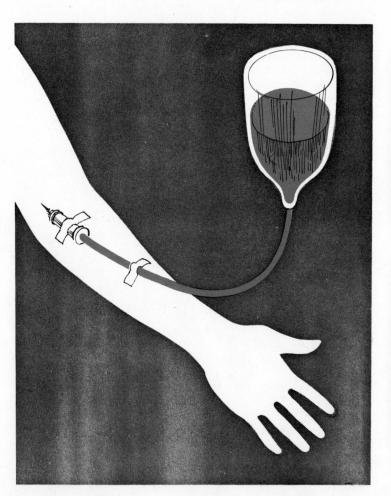
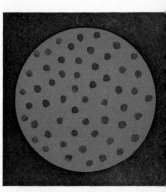
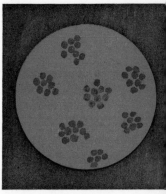

more, it will take so much longer to restore it. So the wise thing to do when a lot of blood has been lost is to give the body help right away. The victim gets what we call a *transfusion,* a "pouring across." Blood can be taken from somebody who is willing to give it and transferred, or "poured across," to the patient. Or it can be taken from a blood bank.

The blood bank is the source mainly used today. It is more convenient. And, besides, just *anybody* who is willing to give blood won't do. Not all blood is the same, and it is important that it should be of the right type. Putting in the wrong blood is worse than putting in none at all. If the wrong type is poured into a patient's blood stream, his plasma may cause the red blood cells in the new blood to clump up or glue together. Then the blood can't get through the capillaries. The wrong type of blood may even kill the patient.

Wrong types of blood killed many people before we learned that blood is not all the same. Dr. Karl Landsteiner taught us that. This was of very great importance during the two World Wars when transfusions were so badly needed for the wounded. Dr. Landsteiner got the Nobel Prize for his great life-saving work.

He discovered that there are four main types of blood. This has nothing to do with the color of a person's skin, or the kind of hair he has, or the shape of his nose. The same four types exist among all the peoples of the world. White men and black men and yellow all have the same four types of blood. The types are called A, B, AB, and O.

Fortunately a great many hospitals in the United States have blood banks today with blood all carefully tested and typed. A doctor can choose just the right blood for his patient. Then the patient's relatives and friends can come to the hospital and give their blood to the bank in exchange for it. That keeps up the supply.

But can blood be stored? Doesn't it spoil?

If it is kept at refrigerator temperature, it won't spoil. But it mustn't be kept long. One reason is that the longer it is kept, the sooner the red blood cells will die when they have been transfused. And old blood causes other problems, too. So what most blood banks do is this. All blood that has not been used up seven days after it was drawn is set aside. Then it is put in a machine and spun around to separate the red cells from the plasma. The red cells are thrown away while the plasma, which contains important chemicals and proteins, is saved. It is frozen and kept to inject into the blood of patients who have suffered shock.

Human blood is so very precious! Couldn't we use animal blood instead?

What a blessing it would be if we could! But it can't be done. Thousands of experiments have been tried to see if one animal's blood could be made to mix with a different animal's. And what was found? If a little blood from a dog, say, was injected into a goat, the dog's red blood cells were destroyed. Only where the animals were very closely related was there no destruction. Man's blood, for example, did no harm when it was injected into an ape.

But who would want to try it the other way around? And where would he get an ape when he needed a transfusion? Or ape's blood? Blood banks stock up only on human blood.

8

White Cells to the Rescue!

We now come to the most exciting solids in the blood. Would anyone suppose that armies of fighters float in the plasma? Would anyone imagine that these warriors march out of the blood stream, attack invading microbes, and fight to the death—kill or be killed?

It sounds fantastic. But it is all true.

In the 1880's, scientists were greatly excited about microbes. Though many people still refused to believe there were such creatures, scientists believed in them. The Russian, Elie Metchnikoff, dreamed of making some great new microbe discovery.

He was living in Sicily in the year 1883. His house was by the shore of the sea and he was studying starfish. Inside the bodies of these animals he had discovered some peculiar white cells. The cells were parts of the creature, and yet they didn't stay in one place like the rest. They wandered all around inside the starfish, moving in a curious way. First they stuck out a part of themselves. Then slowly the rest of the body followed. The cells moved exactly like the one-celled animal called amoeba. They moved by gliding.

White cells can slip out of blood vessels.

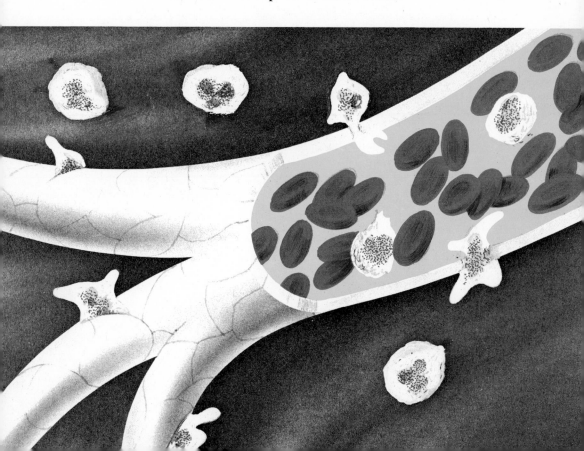

Now, before starfish grow up and become mature, they pass through several stages. While they are larvae, they are transparent. This made it easy for Metchnikoff to study them. When he put a larva under his microscope, he could see everything that went on inside the creature just as if he were looking through a window.

One day the scientist got the idea of sticking little specks of red color inside the larvae. What would the animals do with the red specks? Would they digest them? He was amazed when he saw some of the wandering white cells move up to the bits of red. They flowed right around the red bits and swallowed them up.

A strange thought came to Metchnikoff. Perhaps these white cells that had "eaten" the bits of red would eat microbes, too. Perhaps that was the business of white cells in the starfish. They were to get rid of any substance that didn't by rights belong in the body.

Then a still stranger thought came to him. Perhaps this was the business of white cells in the bodies of human beings, too. Perhaps this was the way human beings got rid of foreign matter and fought microbes. He remembered what happens when a sliver gets into a person's finger. He recalled the pus that often gathers around the sliver.

Metchnikoff at once tried another experiment. He took some rose thorns and stuck them into the body of the starfish larvae. If his thinking was right, then he knew what would happen. The wandering white cells would move towards the thorns and surround them. They would try to get rid of the thorns.

Next morning Dr. Metchnikoff hurried to his microscope. A mass of white wandering cells was all around the thorns. The invaders were being attacked!

Metchnikoff called the white cells *phagocytes,* or "eating cells." Over the years we have learned a good deal about the "eating cells" in our own bodies. We call them *white blood cells,* and there are several kinds. Most of them are twice the size of red blood cells. But, of course, they are still far too small to be seen by the bare eye. Like the red cells, the whites are made inside certain bones, made there by the million, yet not in such quantity as red blood cells. The red cells outnumber the white several hundred to one.

Now, as Metchnikoff saw, the white blood cells have a special power. They can leave the blood stream and go wandering about the body on their own, which is something even the smallest red cell can't do. The white cells are able to do it because they can change their shape.

They slip out between the cells of the thin capillary walls in much the same way that a dog gets through a small hole under a fence. The dog is wider than the hole, but he puts his nose through and starts wiggling. He ·makes himself longer and thinner. He wiggles and wiggles and finally squeezes through. The white cell does the same thing. It pushes a small part of itself between any two cells of the capillary wall, then keeps changing its shape till the whole body has squeezed through. Once out of the capillary, it comes back to its own shape.

But how do the white cells know where to go to find the intruders?

The microbes betray themselves. As soon as they settle down to live in the body, they make a liquid that tells the white cells where the invaders are. The liquid draws the white cells as light attracts moths.

Some of the liquid gets into the nearby capillaries, and that at once alerts the shock troops. The white blood cells begin to slip out, glide towards the enemy, and attack. Each white cell wraps itself around a microbe, then goes after another. The appetite of

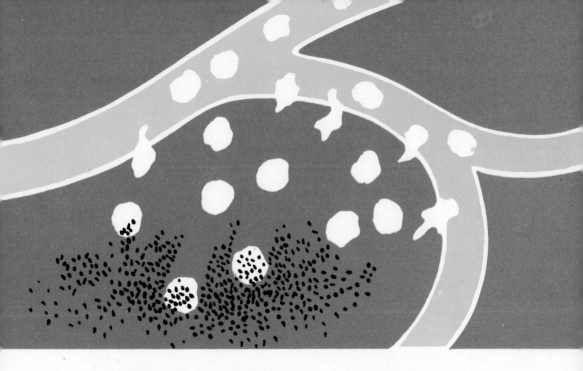

White cells leave the blood stream to surround and destroy invading germs.

the white cells is enormous. A single white cell will swallow alive ten, twenty, thirty or more bacteria. And there the invaders stay till they die. A liquid inside the white cells finally dissolves them.

But after a battle many of the white cells die, too. They get exhausted by the fight. How long a white cell lives depends on how hard it has had to fight. Many are killed in action and live no more than a day. Others, again, may never be called upon to fight at all because during their lifetime no enemy has invaded the body. They may live several months and die merely of old age.

But supposing there is a battle and the white cells don't get the better of the microbes right away? What then?

Then another alarm flashes. More of the liquid has by this time got into the nearby capillaries. At once hundreds more fighters slip out of the bloodstream and glide with all speed to the battlefield. They crowd the part of the body that is threatened by the germs. And a deadly struggle takes place.

Long before this, we may be sure, the owner of the body has felt unwell. Now he is very sick indeed. His temperature has risen to "battle-heat." From 98.6 degrees it has gone up to 101, 102, 103, and is still rising. If the white blood cells manage to eat up the microbes before there get to be too many of them, the patient will recover. But bacteria multiply terribly fast. They simply divide themselves in two. In twelve hours a single bacterium can have as many as a thousand million descendants. The body machine does its best to make more white cells. It sends hundreds of thousands of new fighters into the battle. Yet even so the enemy may beat them down, and the patient may be in for a long illness.

But the battle is not over. There are reserves the body can call up. Antibodies suddenly appear in the blood. The enemy has provoked the body into making new warriors with a remarkable power. These new warriors are chemical fighters. They *combine* with the invaders and make them over into a harmless substance. Or they cause the enemy to clump together so that the white cells can swallow several at a time. Or the antibodies make a poison that kills the invaders. In one way or another the new arrivals act to prevent the microbes from doing any further harm.

It took just four hours for the single germ at top to divide and subdivide into thousands of germs.

9

Dr. Jenner Starts Something

For a long time we have known that if a person has had certain diseases, he will very rarely get them again. A child who has already had the whooping cough can safely be allowed to play with a child who has it. The well child is *immune* to whooping cough, we say. He won't catch it again.

"Why is that?" people used to wonder. They had no idea why it was so. It just was that way.

Today, we are close to the heart of the mystery. At any rate, now that we know about antibodies in the blood, we have a theory about immunity. "When a child has whooping cough," we say, "his body makes antibodies against whooping cough. But it makes more than it needs. So for a long time afterwards some of the antibodies remain in the blood. And when whooping cough bacteria get into his body again, the antibodies destroy them right away. Even before the bacteria have had a chance to multiply."

Everything about immunity is amazing. But the most remarkable part is this: The body makes a *different* antibody against each kind of invader. A child who has had whooping cough is not immune to mumps. He must have mumps before he can become immune to that particular disease.

Now, most adults are protected against measles and chicken pox as well as whooping cough and mumps. They have had all these when they were children and have acquired an immunity against them. The antibodies are still in their blood. But there are many diseases against which we have not acquired immunity. And some of them are dreadful.

Are there no short cuts? Can't we get immunity without having had the disease first?

In some cases we can. We can *provoke* the body to produce the antibodies to protect us. The plan to do it was thought up long ago, before doctors knew anything about antibodies.

A hundred and fifty years back, smallpox was a terrible killer, one of the world's worst. Sometimes entire villages were wiped out by the disease. And when it didn't kill, it left the face all pitted with pockmarks. There were times in Europe when practically everyone had had smallpox. There were times when a woman was called beautiful simply because her face was not scarred.

Sometimes, however, the disease was mild. Fewer people died of it. Fewer were badly scarred. Yet this mild form of smallpox left them just as immune as the severe form. So doctors in the Near East got the idea of purposely bringing on the mild form in order to escape the severe form. Doctors would infect children by taking materials from the sores of a mild case of smallpox and rubbing it into a cut. Most of the children got better and had no scars. But some were badly scarred. Some died. Instead of getting the mild form of the disease, they got the severe one. Parents who let their children be purposely infected took a terrible risk. Yet it seemed a wise choice, and physicians in Europe began to do what doctors in the Near East did.

Now, there was in England a country doctor by the name of Edward Jenner. In his work he saw many dairymaids who had caught *vaccinia,* or cowpox, from the cows they milked. The girls had sores on their hands, arms, and sometimes on their faces. To the doctor the sores looked like smallpox sores, but the girls had no other signs of the disease.

Once a dairymaid said to the doctor, "I cannot get smallpox because I have had cowpox."

Dr. Jenner thought about that. And the next time an epidemic of smallpox broke out, he watched carefully. Many people were desperately sick. But dairymaids who had had the cowpox did not catch smallpox.

"It is certain that vaccinia gives protection against smallpox," the doctor said to himself. But it wasn't enough that he was sure. He had to prove that he was right.

So in the year 1796 he carried out an experiment. He took some material from a cowpox sore on the hand of a dairymaid and rubbed it into a small cut on the arm of an eight year old boy. In a few days a sore appeared, then a scab formed. The boy was scarcely sick before he was better. Six weeks later the doctor infected him with smallpox. And the boy showed no signs of disease. He had become immune to smallpox.

Many wouldn't believe it. Doctors cried out against *vaccination,* as Edward Jenner called his process. But when experiment after experiment proved him right, they stopped doubting. A number of physicians began to protect their patients in the very same way.

Dr. Jenner is so sure that his theory of vaccination will work that he vaccinates a small child.

Today, thanks to Dr. Jenner, we have wiped out smallpox in our country. Not all States have a law that every child must be vaccinated against smallpox. But as no child may enter school unless he has been, it amounts to the same thing. Everybody is protected. And before anyone is allowed to go abroad, he must be vaccinated again, for the protection may not last all through life. Many countries in Europe have practically no smallpox, but there are countries with plenty of it still. In India every year 50,000 people die of the disease. We don't want any of our people to get it abroad. And we certainly don't want them to come back bringing smallpox with them.

10

A Chance Discovery

Immunity is full of surprises. The children in a family may all be down with the measles, yet the newborn baby doesn't catch it. He is immune to measles, for his mother's antibodies are in his blood.

Sooner or later, alas! he is bound to fall prey to microbes because his first blessed immunity won't remain with him long. But science can give him lots of protection today. For that wonder of wonders, Man, has not hauled down the flag. He has not yielded to the invisible enemies that live at the expense of mankind. Around the year 1880, the great French scientist Louis Pasteur learned that microbes can be tamed. And a whole chain of triumphant discoveries followed from that.

Pasteur made his discovery, as so often happens, just by chance. He was working on chicken cholera, a disease of fowls, and was having problems and difficulties. He got so impatient at last that he decided to go off on vacation. And then, just before he left, a strange thing happened.

A flask of deadly chicken cholera microbes had been put away in the laboratory and forgotten. Now the flask was brought out, and Pasteur's helpers

Pasteur vaccinates a child in his laboratory. The shepherds (left), who were bitten by a wolf, await their turn.

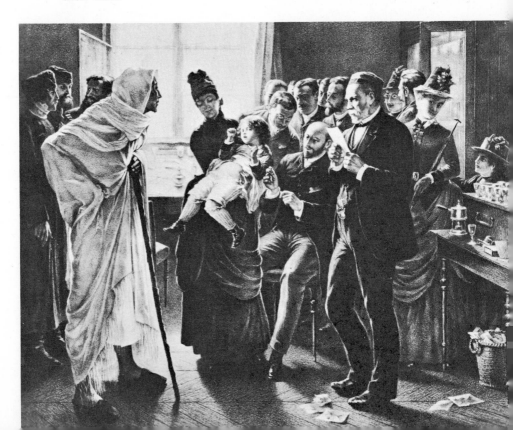

inoculated some chickens with the microbes. As fully expected, the birds got sick. But next morning, lo and behold! They were cackling away as contentedly as ever.

What was wrong? Why didn't the chickens die? Still puzzling over the riddle, Pasteur went away on his holiday.

It was when he returned that the miracle happened. The chickens that had been inoculated with the old microbes were brought into the laboratory again and shot full of fresh, deadly microbes. And to everyone's astonishment, the birds stayed perfectly well.

Chance had disclosed a great secret to Louis Pasteur. And by good fortune his mind was prepared to receive it. He grasped that the first lot of microbes had grown weak by being exposed for a long time to the air. In a flash he remembered Dr. Jenner. Vaccination! He himself had now

accidentally stumbled on the same process. He had *vaccinated* the chickens. The weakened microbes were a vaccine!

Pasteur grew dizzy thinking about the wonderful future ahead of him. Doubtless it was possible to make a vaccine for every germ disease in the world if one could find a way of weakening the microbes. There was anthrax now. Anthrax was killing flock after flock of sheep in France. Could he make a vaccine for anthrax? What a thing it would be for French farmers if he succeeded!

Pasteur did succeed. He astonished all France with his anthrax vaccine. Then he made a vaccine for rabies, the dread disease that makes dogs mad— and makes mad the human beings whom the rabid dogs bite. With that victory he stirred the world. Nineteen peasants who had been bitten by a mad wolf came to him from far-away Russia. Pasteur saved them—all but three.

Other scientists picked up from there. They worked out vaccines for a whole string of diseases— diphtheria, tetanus, typhoid, yellow fever, typhus, influenza. Last of all Dr. Jonas Salk added polio serum to the list. We all know about that one. We've all had the shots.

Some of the vaccines contain weakened microbes. Some contain dead ones. And some have in them the weakened poison which the microbes make. Each is different, yet all work the same way. They all provoke the body to make antibodies, and the antibodies in the blood make the body immune.

Surprised girl discovers it doesn't hurt a bit!

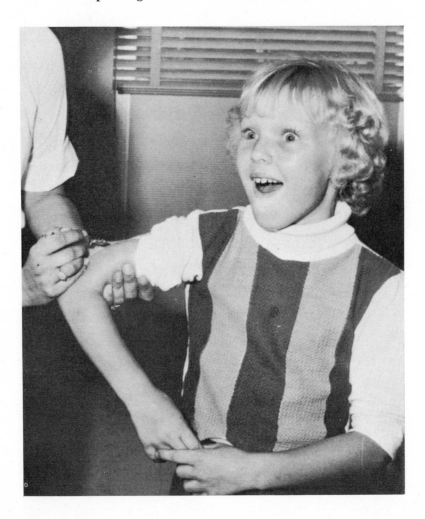

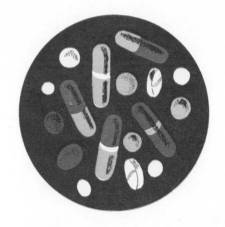

11
Miracle Drugs

In olden days men dreamed of finding a wonder-working stone. The "philosopher's stone" they called it. They believed that if they had this magic thing, they would be able to change base metals into silver and gold.

Today no one worries about changing tin and lead into silver and gold. Scientists are busy with far more important research. They have a thousand worthier projects. And among them the most worth-while is finding ways of helping the body to fight disease.

"Wouldn't it be wonderful," we say, "if we could be protected against every germ disease in the world! Wouldn't it be grand if one shot could make us immune to all the deadly microbes!"

It would indeed. And perhaps it really *is* possible to make an antibody that would be able to destroy every microbe that plagues us. Scientists are working on the idea. But there are great difficulties in the way. Bacteria are such tiny things—25,000 medium-sized ones would just about cover the dot we use for a period. As for antibodies, they are so small that if you divided an inch into two million parts, an antibody would be the size of one and a half of those parts. Each kind is different in some small way, and what the meaning of these small differences is, we don't understand. What is more, antibodies are proteins, and we don't know how to make proteins. We don't know the formula for any of them. So it looks as if for a very long time to come we will have to depend on our own antibodies in the blood.

But isn't there another way? Couldn't we find a chemical or a drug that would make us immune?

Impossible. Scientists throw up their hands when you suggest such a thing. They would be satisfied to find a way of killing the various microbes once they got into the body. It is simple enough to kill them in the laboratory. Heat will do it, though it takes several hours of boiling to kill some. Chemicals will do it. But the problem is to find chemicals or drugs that will kill the microbes without hurting the body. It's not much use to give a patient a drug that will kill him as well as the microbes.

For a long time there was just one microbe-destroying drug that doctors could use. It was quinine. We learned about it from the American Indians. It was used to treat malaria. Later on, drugs were developed to cure most of the tropical diseases. Then in the 1930's we got the sulfa drugs.

Indians made quinine from certain tree barks.

They act on certain round microbes that destroy red blood cells and cause "blood poisoning." The sulfa drugs keep the bacteria from multiplying. They make it possible for the white cells to conquer them.

A great sigh of relief went up when the sulfa drugs first came on the market. Deaths of mothers in childbirth and of patients sick with pneumonia and of soldiers suffering from wounds went way down. But now the most powerful weapons the doctors have against these same round microbes are the antibiotics. They are not chemicals. Antibiotics are made from living things that have the power to *kill* bacteria. Quite a few of us have had experience with one of these latest miracle drugs—penicillin.

Penicillin is made from a mold that came floating in through a laboratory window in London one day in the year 1928 and settled on a plateful of bacteria. Dr. Alexander Fleming was carefully growing those bacteria. When he found his garden moldy, the doctor was disgusted. He was about to throw the mess away when he noticed something strange. All around the place where the mold had settled, the bacteria had disappeared. And for some inches beyond the empty ring, his bacteria garden had become transparent. Now this was so strange that

Dr. Fleming decided not to throw the mold away.
He would save it and grow it in a test tube.

It was a lucky thing for mankind that he did.
For that penicillium mold proved to be a most
powerful killer of many of the most murderous
bacteria in the world. Today when anyone is sick

**Dr. Fleming, discoverer of penicillin, at work in
his laboratory.**

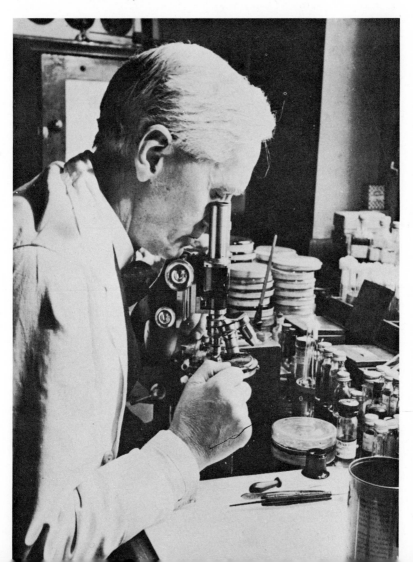

with a strep throat, or pneumonia, or "blood poison-ing," a doctor is almost sure to rely on penicillin to pull his patient through.

"The world is so full of a number of things," scientists say—and feel as happy as kings. For they believe that if molds will kill bacteria, there must be other humble natural killers. A whole new world is theirs to explore.

And they are exploring it—eagerly, with devotion, with excitement. Already they have come up with a few more miracle drugs. In time they are bound to find others.

And we, of course, shall greet every discovery with joy and applause. For what could be more welcome? The human body is the most wonderful machine in the world. Nothing is more amazing than the blood's white cells in action, or the antibodies the body sends to the blood as its last line of defense. But our invisible enemies are many and powerful. They cling to life as hard as we do. Anything that helps us defeat them is a blessing. Anything that helps is a triumph for Man.

c.2

612   White, Anne Terry
White   Secrets of the heart and blood

B 11-875